Hen Nights

...and other great nights out with the girls!

Created by
Sonya Winner & Ilana Salem

Thank you to:
Judith and Adam Apter, Colin Bowling, Julia and Philip Burton, Charlie Carmen, John Catto, Charles Cordell, Mike Dawson, Lydia Drukarz, Stephen Fisher, Paul Forrester, Andrew Franklin, Ruth and Harold Glickman, Ingrid and Andy Goodman, Tim Jackson, Anna Josse, Neville and Susan Kahn, Jeannette Kupferman, Dee Lahiri, Katie Mierens, Laura Morris, Moss Bros, Tony Mulliken, Mysteries, Simon Olswang Louise Peters, John Pickard, Natasha Pollard, Claudia and Gina Pollinger, Charles Salem, Claudette and Elliot Salem, Ann Summers, Elizabeth Sutton-Klein, Abner Stein, Daniel Tasker, Ruth Thompson, Lex van Dam, Gozi Wamuo, Barry Winkleman, Daniel Winner and Mary Winner and Paul Winner.

First published in 1999 by André Deutsch Limited
76 Dean Street
London W1V 5HA
http://www.vci.co.uk
André Deutsch is a subsidiary of VCI plc

A catalogue record for this book is available from the British Library
ISBN 0 233 99484 X Printed in Belgium

Credits:
Created by Sonya Winner and Ilana Salem
Written by Ilana Salem
Design, Art Direction and Co-ordination by Sonya Winner
Hen illustrations by Rachael Busch
Photomontage by Sonya Winner using Adobe Photoshop 5
Gift illustrations by Jacqueline Nicholls
Photography by Colin Bowling and James Johnson
Modelling by Natasha Pollard
Edited by Anna Kiernan and Louise Dixon

To Amber

for your Hen Night

Dear Chief Hen,

Everyone knows that organizing your best mate's night out is a heavy responsibility. But do not fear, help is at hand in the form of our essential, definitive guide to Hen Nights.

Let us help you make this a fun, memorable and successful experience. We've covered all types of Hen:

The Posh Hen

The Shy and Retiring Hen

The Cultured Hen

The New Age Hen *and*

The Outrageously Wild Hen

We've also devised other great nights out for each kind of girl. What's more, there are success and disaster stories told by real live Hens, plus great ideas for Hen presents and the Essential Directory of entertainment, transport, tailor-made weekends. In fact everything you'll need to make you have a night to remember.

Enjoy, and Happy Hentertaining!

What type of Hen?

What should you do?

National Trust house
Karaoke – it's a hoot!
A murder mystery party
Studs and polo
Indulgences and pampering
Walkie talkies
Come dancing
Game for anything
Flower shower
Thespian's dream
Gastronomic delights
Go green

A superb performance
Day at the races
Massage and muscles
Futuristic fun
Mind games
Potty about pottery
Balloon odyssey
Fun-fair frolics
Everybody's going surfing
White knuckle rafting
What's your fetish?
Wild West...

The Do's & Don'ts of Hen Nights

Do give yourself enough time to organize the event. Remember everyone's diary is always choc-a-bloc with arrangements.

Do consult the bride-to-be on whom she wants to invite. It may not be her wish for work colleagues or future family to be at such an intimate event.

Do liaise with the bride as to what she has in mind. You don't want your Hen to barricade herself in the loo for the whole evening when she sees a g-string-clad strippogram arrive.

Do tell everyone to bring a small gift, whether sexy, funny or reminiscent of past events.

Don't rely on the other guests to invite people. You're the organizer, so do the job.

Don't forget that everyone's on a budget so let everyone know roughly what the damage is going to be.

Don't forget your camera/camcorder. It's great to have a permanent reminder of the event.

Don't get personal with the Hen about her new groom. She may not want the world knowing about the details of her sex life. Talking about exes is fine though!

POSH HEN

Engaged to a William, Nigel or Sebastian. A Hen from excellent stock. Parents have at least three homes, including a 'Hice in the Cantry'. Her laughter is punctuated with lots of snorting and 'Oh darlings'. Nails, skin, hair and clothes always look immaculate. Knickers and bra always match. Never farts in public although may admit to the odd 'bottom burp' behind closed doors.

Works in PR or for a well-known charity. Lets her hair down with a couple of bottles of Bolly. Has access to an endless trust fund but won't discuss it as it's rather tasteless to be flash, darling... Suffice to say, her wedding will be a real event. Look out for coverage in the glossies.

Organizing POSH Hen Nights

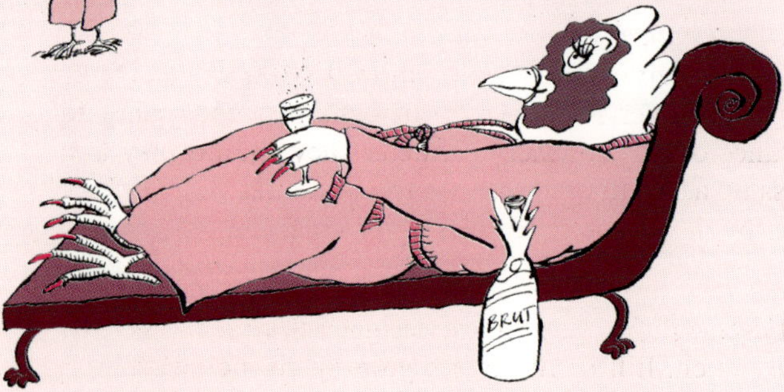

National Trust house, darling!

If it's a Summer Hen Do, why not go for a gourmet picnic at the National Trust house of your choice, and pretend you're Helena Bonham-Carter in a Merchant Ivory film. Don't wear your best frock as it may get grass stained! If it's winter time, pretend you're Henry VIII and hold a banquet in an 'olde worlde' pub steeped in local interest with a real fire smouldering in the hearth.

Karaoke – it's a hoot!

Force your Posh Hen out of her upper-crust reserve with a Karaoke night. Make sure she and all the other guests have a go and if you all get a bit blotto try rewriting the lyrics so they're more suggestive. Remember, nobody could sing as badly as Cameron Diaz in *My Best Friend's Wedding!*

Gosh! A murder mystery party

Buy, make up or go to an organized *Whodunnit Murder Mystery* dinner party. Send out details to each guest in advance detailing which character they should play and dress up as on the evening. At the best ones you won't be able to tell who's a guest and who's an actor!

Studs and polo

Get dressed up in your finest designer clothes and go to a polo match. It'll be fun to see yummy, fit men with their jodhpurs on showing what they're made of. Hang around the stables if you want to get a closer look at their assets.

Indulgences and pampering

Gather together a group of your favourite girlies and hit the local health farm. Just lounge about in dressing gowns having every conceivable treatment possible and come back a whole new you. If nothing else, your feet will have a chance of looking good on your honeymoon!

Shy & Retiring HEN

This Hen is a real homebird and is never happier than when she's cuddling up with a good book and plenty of hot chocolate. Friends describe her as 'a really nice girl'. She wears a lot of beige, always with a pair of sensible Hush Puppies. She works as a researcher or behind-the-scenes in something. Every Christmas for the past five years her boss has asked her if she's just joined the company.

∞

Loves listening to late night radio phone-ins but never dares phone in herself. Favourite expression is, 'How embarrassing!' which is usually accompanied by a red rash creeping up her neck. Wedding likely to be a low-key affair in a church hall or similar. Needless to say, she is dreading every minute of it. Her dress will be very plain and she may, if feeling daring, wear a smattering of peach lipstick.

HOT CHOCOLA
Wuthering Heights
EMILY BRONTË

Organizing *Shy & Retiring* Hen Nights

Walkie talkies

Shy and Retiring types usually like to do quite solitary things like walking or rambling. Walks can be up to ten miles per day and include coastal walking with time to stop and stare and take in the atmosphere. The leader can point out local heritage, myths and legends. Bring walking boots and wet weather clothes and a few hip flasks.

Come dancing

Why not help your Hen come out of her shell a bit with a dancing lesson? Choose from folk, tap, jazz, ballroom, Latin American, or even line dancing! It might liven things up a bit at the wedding if you get everyone from the village vicar to her mother-in-law joining in the line!

Horsing around

If she's a horsey type she might like to do something like pony-trekking, which can be organized with stop-offs at local pubs, and even an overnight stay at a B & B. You could make it real fun by having a treasure hunt en route, picking up all sorts of saucy presents to help your Hen get into the spirit of things.

Game for anything

Have a cards or Scrabble evening. Once you start playing and competing you won't be able to stop. Set dares for the losing team like getting the man in the local off-licence to give you some free booze, or stop a policeman and ask him to take down your particulars!

Flower shower

Take her on a flower-arranging day. At least she won't have to make conversation with the carnations and she might even pick up a few tips for the wedding.

Cultured HEN

Came out of the womb singing Vivaldi's 'Spring'. Recited Chaucer from a very early age. Lives for classical concerts, opera, plays by obscure South American playwrights. Occasionally succumbs to listening to popular music – but only in the car. Wears very classical designer clothes, a little too old for her. Never goes to the theatre without a copy of the text under her arm. Intellectual snob. A member of the local operatic society, she appreciates fine wines, fine music and fine food. Met her fiancé in an art gallery. Nearly split up because he expressed the view that Picasso is overrated.

Dinner conversations at her place are on impressionism, existentialism and hatred of materialism. Wedding likely to be tasteful, with endless speeches peppered with literary quotations. Drink plenty to avoid dying of boredom.

THE
MERRY
WIDOW

Organizing *Cultured* Hen Nights

Thespian's dream

Many Cultured Hens are really frustrated luvvies, so a short break to Shakespeare's birthplace would be ideal. You could see performances at the Royal Shakespeare Theatre and have intimate discussions with the cast. Afterwards, you could always let your hair down with a night out in Stratford.

Gastronomic delights

Go on a gourmet away-day or weekend break. Either find something organized in a country house hotel or take a great cook away with you. Agree beforehand the kind of scrummies you want on the menu and then sit back with a glass of wine or five and your fork at the ready.

Go green

If your Hen's keen on creating a beautiful garden for poetry recitals, then take her off to a one day gardening course to find out which plants and materials to use. She may even get into growing her own organic produce, to serve with glasses of Champers at her literary evenings!

A superb performance

Hire a box at the opera, theatre or local concert hall to see your Hen's favourite performance of all time. Prepare some delicious homemade canapés, sandwiches and truffles for the interval, and try to divert your Cultured Hen away from analysing the text.

Day at the races

Get your glad rags on, take out plenty of dosh from your bank account and have a flutter at the races. If your horse comes in, you could get a nest egg to set you up for the future.

new age HEN

A millennium hippy. Never without a joss-stick in hand. Thinks Fleetwood Mac's 'Rumours' album is still hip. Wears floaty hippy clothes and thermal underwear. Her life is ruled by the full moon and ascending star signs. Hobbies include yoga and aromatherapy and she is presently doing a shiatsu massage course. She tells everyone she has healing powers. Likely to say, 'In life, what goes around comes around'.

♋

Friends will be served tofu, alfalfa, beansprouts, organic vegetables, fruit and herbal tea. No chance of ever getting a choccy biscuit. Ambition is to have a flotation tank in her bedsit. Met current husband-to-be at the bottle bank. Impressed by his 'Meat is Murder' T-shirt and 2CV. Wedding likely to be totally vegetarian, hopefully with more than one loo on site.

Massage and muscles

Have an evening of massage. Ring up two hunky, male masseurs and get them round to your flat with oils and plenty of energy, to give each of the Hens an hour's worth of muscle pummelling. Afterwards, you could get a professional make-up artist round to make each of you up, then go for a wild night on the town as the new you!

Futuristic Fun

Go to a seance, crystal ball or palm reader. It's bound to be on the list of your New Age Hen's ambitions. Just hope she doesn't take it too seriously by calling off the wedding if the future doesn't look too rosy!

Mind games

Go for a day of yoga and improve your mind, body and spirit through exercise and meditation. You'll learn breathing techniques and lots of weird and wonderful positions that might even make your Hen more exciting in the bedroom!

Potty about pottery

Indulge her fantasies of having her own pottery studio in the back garden and take her on a one day pottery course. You'll learn how to throw, hand build, turn and fire a kiln. Just think of Demi Moore in *Ghost* and imagine all those naughty shapes you could create after you've had a few!

Balloon odyssey

Feel like floating close to heaven without a care in the world? Then why not take her ballooning – either in the daytime or, if it's a glorious summer's evening, at night. Ideal if you're planning a Hen Do of five or under but make sure you don't drink too much before the flight!

Outrageously Wild HEN

One place you'll never find her is at home. Always expect to get the answer machine. Says exactly what she thinks. Does everything for maximum attention. Speaks in a very loud voice and has an extremely raucous laugh that's recognizable a mile away. Works in advertising or in the music business. Favourite expression: 'You've got to live life dangerously', before downing seven tequila slammers.

Loves clubbing and watching Teletubbies completely stoned at seven in the morning. Has outrageous dress sense and loves vivid colours. Wedding likely to be completely over the top, much to the embarrassment of her parents-in-law. She's dying to show all the guests her black stretchy underwear. Bound to mention all 32 ex-boyfriends in her wedding speech, if she stays sober enough to deliver it. Definitely won't be wearing white.

Fun-fair frolics

Head for your local theme park, no matter how few rides they have, and go on the big dipper, waltzer, helter skelter, carousel and ghost train as if you were sweet sixteen again. Eat candy floss, sticks of rock, nasty hamburgers and chips washed down with plenty of lager, then throw up all over the no.12 bus on the way back home.

Everybody's going surfing

Who can resist seeing hunky men in skimpy surf suits? Surfing is one of the most exhilarating and fun sports you could try your hand at. Weekend courses are available from April to October for beginners, with a great choice of local pubs and clubs, plus barbecues and brawn on the beach.

White knuckle rafting

Fancy tackling some of Britain's most demanding white waters in the safety and stability of a large inflated raft? Rafting usually lasts four hours and covers 15 miles of exciting moving water. It's an exhilarating experience which offers a great excuse to get completely sloshed afterwards. All specialist equipment is provided.

What's your fetish?

There are hundreds of fetish clubs around Britain where you can indulge your deepest fantasies. Go dressed in rubber, bondage, leather or PVC and get ready to be severely disciplined if you fall out of line. Not for the squeamish or faint-hearted!

Wild West

Satisfy your Hen's insatiable appetite with a Wild West stud. Take her line dancing to see how many cowboys she can mount before she gets well and truly hitched.

Real life Hen *DISASTER* stories

Everyone wants their Hen Night to be a success but unfortunately it doesn't always go so smoothly. Here are some examples from real live Hens on how it can all go horribly wrong!

Julia from Epsom writes...

I had just seen the film Withnail and I about two guys who have a fairly wild time in a country cottage, which inspired me to organize a Hen weekend at a remote cottage in Dorset. I had planned it with military precision. We would be driving down from London on a Friday night and collecting the keys from a farmer who lived nearby.

We arrived, as promised, before 10 pm, in the pitch dark, only to find the farm in complete darkness too. There was nobody at home and here we were, six girls in two cars wearing skimpy summer clothes as the weather turned colder. At first we were in hysterics but after 10 minutes reality set in and we started to panic about taking out our contact lenses and having a shower. After spending a futile hour looking for any nearby B & Bs, we ended up having to spend the night in a field in our cars .

None of us had any camping experience and we quickly had to get used to peeing over a bed of thistles. The next morning we woke up screaming at the sight of a herd of bulls nuzzling up to the car windows. Later we received a call from the farmer's neighbour who told us that he had had an accident that day and had had to spend the night in hospital.

And the moral of the story is...

Have a map of the area with alternative accommodation listed or you may end up shacking up in the back of a car à la *Thelma and Louise.*

Claire from Barnsley writes...

It was my friend Judith's Hen Night and it was quite difficult for me to put a list of friends together for the big night because I'd moved away to another town and didn't know her friends that well.

I cobbled together what I thought was the perfect list and we arranged to meet at the local Thai restaurant for karaoke and fun. Judith walked in, took one look at the gaggle of Hens, turned bright red and fled to the loo in a flurry of tears.

After banging on the door for five minutes while she sobbed hysterically, I eventually found out that she had recently discovered one of her so-called best mates shagging her fiancé in the changing rooms at the local gym. Evidently he had wanted a quick fling before the wedding and Judith's friend had obliged.

Judith refused to come out of the loo until the said horny Hen had left the table. After some time she walked back into the restaurant with her mascara-stained face forcing a welcoming smile. Everyone tried hard to be jolly but couldn't hide their feelings of embarrassment.

And the moral of the story is...

Go over the invitation list with your Hen before the Hen Night to save any embarrassing moments.

Anna from Birmingham writes...

Here's a classic case of total disorganization and miscommunication. You need the exact opposite of these two things if you want your Hen Night to be a success. I was organizing a Hen Night for my best friend Karen and made the fatal mistake of not consulting her beforehand about who she would like to come. I assumed that she wanted to invite her future mother-in-law, grandmother and sister-in-law, so I just went ahead and invited them.

At first Karen had wanted something really low-key in a restaurant nearby but then, at the last minute, she changed her mind and decided to meet at Ann Summers in Soho, followed by a night at Madame JoJo's – a transvestite club. As the organizer I had remembered to inform all twelve Hens about the change in venue but had forgotten to cancel the family group.

Unbeknown to me, they were getting a lift with Karen's sister – you can imagine their faces when they walked into Ann Summers to see Karen and all her tartily-clad friends fooling around with vibrators and an assortment of sex aids.

The group dressed in twin-sets and pearls walked out in disgust, swiftly followed by an apologetic and shocked looking Karen trying to appease them.

And the moral of the story is...

Don't invite members of your Hen's family unless you are sure that nothing embarrassing has been arranged.

Real life

Hen Success stories

Some Hen Nights just have everything going for them. Usually it's because there's a fine flock of friends who just want to have fun and let their feathers down!

Suzannah from Cheshire writes...

I organized a very different kind of Hen Night for my best friend, Emma. I decided to get together her five ex-boyfriends to celebrate her last night of singledom. I should mention that Emma is a psychologist so there was a very good chance that she would observe this as a great study of human behaviour.

The evening was a scream from start to finish. Each ex introduced himself in the exact order of when Emma went out with him. Each script ended with things like, 'And I was chucked for the very handsome Steve sitting on my right who she met at the cricket club'. The rapport between the guys was brilliant, as none of them had hard feelings and each one had, unusually, remained very good friends with Emma.

There were some excellent anecdotes about Emma's strange bedtime habits and of course lots of digs between the guys saying things like, 'So you're the smart-arsed lawyer who she chucked me for, and you're not even that good looking!'

At the end of the evening each ex had written a hilarious limerick about going out with Emma, which I had framed for her. They also brought really appropriate presents for her that gave everyone a good laugh. She still maintains it was one of the most entertaining, yet touching, evenings she has ever spent and her fiancé was totally relaxed about it too.

And the moral of the story is...
Ask your Hen before contacting all her exes.
Also make sure that her fiancé's ego can handle it!

Roz from Wales writes...

My sister, Samantha, is a real fitness freak, so I thought going on one of these Outward Bound courses was ideal for her. Thirteen of us piled into four cars and headed for the centre.

On Saturday night we all went out for a conventional celebration meal and indulged in some drinking and dancing. The fun part was that we had organized a lucky dip from which Sam pulled out unwrapped gifts, ranging from practical things like massage creams and hair dye to saucier stuff like chocolate willies and 'naughty' drinking straws.

The next morning it was up early for the army training course. It was a real case of the survival of the fittest. We began with water-sliding, which involved sliding down a huge sheet of plastic laid down a massive slope, and as each of us slid down we were hosed from top to bottom. It was like a scene from 'It's a Knockout!'

After that, we went grass sledging which involved us mounting tiny sledges with very small wheels which went ridiculously fast down hills. After lunch we split into two groups and had to make a raft, which we then had to race in and afterwards dismantle.

Climbing up a fifteen foot high pole then jumping on to a trapeze was the scariest thing of all, but fortunately there was a safety net and we were harnessed up for it. All in all it was a really exhilarating challenge and a real exercise in team building.

And the moral of the story is...

Choose something that's a real challenge and it's bound to be a unique and unforgettable experience.

Kate from Dumfries writes...

My Hen Night was superbly organized by my cousin. All my girlfriends are big drinkers and serious clubbers but we didn't want the drag of driving from club to club, so she organized a limousine to chauffeur us around.

There are lots of limo companies that cater for parties of six to twelve. There were ten of us girlies all dressed up to the nines, sipping chilled champagne out of silver ice buckets in the back of the car. We felt like Hollywood movie stars, especially as we got some amazing attention from guys because we had organized VIP passes into all the clubs. We would just pull up in front of a club, pass all the people who were queueing outside and go straight in.

My friends had also made up a tape of all my favourite smoochy songs which we played in the back of the car.

We had a camcorder with us to record all the highlights of the evening which we took with us into all the clubs. The evening ended with us piling into the back of the car with a few hunky blokes and we watched the camcorder film of the evening on the video before being dropped off home.

It certainly went down as a night to remember, and at least I can say I know how Cher feels!

And the moral of the story is...
Do something on your Hen Night that makes you feel like a star!

heavenly hen presents

Here are some tame prezzie suggestions to treat your Hen to, and give her a real good send-off before her big day.

Glamorous

Earrings, brooches, necklaces, bracelets, matching jewellery sets with engraving to commemorate her Hen Night.

Gardening

Subscription to gardening mag, seeds, trees and shrubs to plant in commemoration of Hen's marriage.

Food

Case of wine from year of marriage, subscription to cookery magazine or chocolate society, chocolate initials of bride and groom-to-be.

Memories

Silver photo frame complete with picture of Hen's friends mounted in a frame, or make up your own album of the Hen night or wedding, for her to keep forever.

Floral
Modern dried flower arrangements, arranged bouquets, pot pourri, vase.

Accessories
Shawl, scarf, leather gloves, handbag, waistcoat, hair accessories.

Home Comforts
Heart-shaped hot water bottle, novelty slippers, supper tray.

Smelly Stuff
Aromatherapy oils, bubble bath, perfume, body spray, essential travel set especially for honeymoons!

Alternative
Candle holder, scented candle, wind chime, joss-sticks, lavender scented pillow, Bach flower remedies for wedding nerves!

Girlie

Lingerie, negligé, manicure/pedicure set, jewellery roll/box, tissue holder, make-up bag with her favourite brand of make-up.

Personal

Personalized stationery, diary, key ring, purse, dinner party book, guest book.

Literary

Glam coffee table book, love poems, erotic prose, jokey book, loo book or yearly subscription to Hen's favourite girlie mag.

Music

CD, CD carrier, cassette player, Walkman, Discman, concert tickets. Make a request on the radio and tape it, or make up a cassette of your Hen's most raunchy tunes and introduce each track.

Hellish
Hen Presents

Here are
some really
wicked prezzie
suggestions to treat
your Hen to. Start the
bride blushing before she's
even begun her wedding day!

Tame him!

Mistress mask, leather whip, dog collar, plastic handcuffs, schoolboy cane.

Bodily Pleasures

Smelly creams to increase sensitivity and intensify orgasm. Lickable and scented massage lotion. Herbal potion containing aphrodisiacs, or design your very own erotic blend of oils and give it an apt name.

Off the Wall

Dreamy calendar of your sexiest men to salivate over. Make up your own 'Countdown to the wedding' calendar with funny personal messages to your Hen.

Blow Jobbies

Inflatable Toy Boy to take to parties when your man's off on a business trip.

Naughty Exec Fun

Dirty doodle pad, willy notepad, penis pencil top, keyring, willy stress buster to squeeze very hard when you're frustrated!

Jewellery for your Jangles!

Colourful lightweight adjustable aluminium nipple chain.

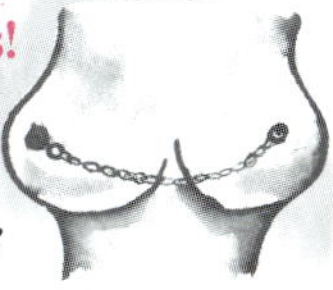

Body Beautiful

Temporary tattoos, edible chocolate body paint, fruit-flavoured condoms, edible wild fruit body paint, delay spray for his wanton willy.

Sex Vibes!

Vibrators with different names and functions. Choose from big black ones, flesh-coloured ones, silver and gold ones, red hot or knobbly ones or even ones that look like corn on the cob!

Privates on Parade!

Animal pouches – crocodile pouch, giraffe pouch, flasher pouch, snapper pouch or make up your own relevant animal. Big willy cheeky boxer shorts, horny devil socks.

Titivating T-shirts for Her

T-shirt with your own made-up saucy statements with the date and location printed on it, e.g. 'I'm on Sue's Hen Night'.

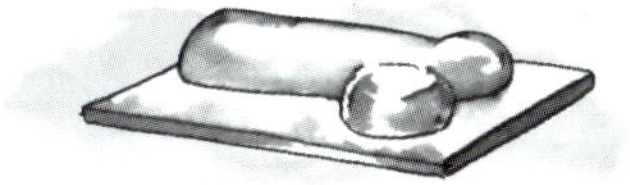

Edible Delights

Liquorice flavoured bikini briefs or bra, willy-shaped pasta, phallic-shaped jelly mould.

Bathtime Fun!

Willy-shaped soap, naughty back scratcher that reaches all your naughty parts, vibrating bath massage ball.

Cock-Tail Presents!

Willy shaped straws, willy ice cube holders, nude male bottle opener.

Sexy Seductress

PVC padded bra, thong and suspender belt, peephole bra, crotchless knickers, fishnet stockings, basque, teddie, crotchless tights.

Book Worms

Kama Sutra, How to Make Love to the Same Person for the Rest of Your Life, Sex Maniac's Cook Book, Sexy Cocktail Book, 227 Ways to Unleash the Sex Goddess in Every Woman, Men are from Mars, Women are from Venus.

HOLLYWOOD 'quotes'

In Tinsel Town marriage is still very much the done thing. The problem is how many times they do it! Here's what the stars say about love and the Big M!

'In Hollywood all marriages are happy. It's trying to live together afterwards that causes the problems.'
Shelly Winters

'Some women pick men to marry and others pick them to pieces.'
Mae West

'A successful man is one who makes more money than his wife can spend. A successful woman is one who can find such a man.'
Lana Turner

'Never give a man back his diamonds.'
Zsa Zsa Gabor

'The trouble with some women is that they get all excited about nothing and then marry him.'
Cher

'My idea of superwoman is someone who scrubs her own floors.'
Bette Midler

'I hate housework! You make the beds, you do the dishes and six months later you have to start all over again.'
Joan Rivers

'Too much of a good thing can be wonderful.'
Mae West

Glossary

Here are some classic cockney phrases to thrill your Hen with on the night or use in the Best Man's wedding speech. Either way, you'll find they give you a real Cow and Calf – Laugh!

Skinny as a Broom .... Groom

Mother's Pride .... Bride

Light of My Life .... Wife

Pot and Pan .... Man

Joy Stick .... Prick

Gay and Frisky .... Whisky

Kermit the Frog .... Bog

Laurel and Hardy .... Bacardi

Oedipus Rex .... Sex

Rise and Shine .... Wine

Russell Harty .... Party

Saint and Sinner .... Dinner

Scotch Mist .... Pissed

Snow Whites .... Tights

Daily Express .... Dress

Yorkshire Rippers .... Slippers

Here it is... The definitive guide to every Hen activity. We've also included companies specializing in tailor-made Hen Weekends, as well as details of where to get your Hen present.

There are also some great websites worth visiting, for all you surfing Hens out there. A great starting point for your web searches is at www.leisurehunt.com/, *where you will find a wealth of information on accommodation, culture, eating and drinking, nature, sport, and travel throughout the UK and abroad.*

Activities

Abseiling:

British Mountaineering Council
177/179 Burton Road,
Manchester M20 2BB
Tel: 0161 445 4747
Fax: 0161 445 4500

Adventure Courses:

If you're looking for a 1-5 day multi-activity break then the following suggestions are ideal. They cover a huge variety of activities like archery, abseiling, caving, pot holing, mountain biking, canoeing, orienteering and white water rafting.

Acorn Activities
PO Box 120, Hereford HR4 8YB
Tel: 01432 830083
Fax: 01432 830110
www.acornactivities.co.uk

Anglian Activity
29 Yarmouth Road,
Norwich NR7 OED
Tel: 01603 700 770
Fax: 01603 701 166
www.anglianactivities.co.uk

The Adventure Company
Low Grove Farm,
Millbeck,
Keswick,
Cumbria CA12 4PS
Tel: 017687 75351
Fax: 017687 75763
E-mail:sales@theadventureco.com
www.theadventureco.com

Black Mountain Activities
PO Box 5,
Hay-on-Wye
Herefordshire HR3 5YB
Tel/Fax: 01497 847 897
E-mail:enquires@blackmountain.co.uk
www.blackmountain.co.uk

Edale YHA Activity Centre
Rowland Cote, Nether Booth,
Edale, Hope Valley S33 7ZH
Tel: 014336 70302
www.yha-englandwales.org.uk

Great Glen School of Adventure
Great Glen Water Park,
South Laggan, Spean Bridge,
Inverness-shire PH34 4EA
Tel: 01809 501 381
Fax: 01809 501 218

HF Holidays Ltd
Imperial House, Edgware Road,
London NW9 5AL
Tel: 0181 905 9557
Fax: 0181 205 0506
E-mail:101523.1274@compuserve.com

Outdoor Adventure
Atlantic Court,Widemouth Bay,
Bude, Cornwall EX23 0DF
Tel: 01288 361 312
Fax: 01288 361 153
E-mail:info@outdooradventure. co.uk
www.outdooradventure.co.uk

Outward Bound
Watermillock, Penrith,
Cumbria CA11 0JL
Tel: 0990 134227
Fax: 017684 86983
www.outwardbound-uk.org

Airsports

The British Hang-Gliding and Paragliding Association
The Old Schoolroom,
Loughborough Road,
Leicester LE4 5PJ
Tel: 01162 611 322
Fax: 01162 611 323
www.bhpa.co.uk

Archery

Grand National Archery Society
Seventh Street,
National Agricultural Centre,
Stoneleigh, Kenilworth
Warwickshire CV8 2LG
Tel: 01203 696 631
Fax: 01203 419 662
www.gnas.u-net.com

Assault Courses

The Outdoor Trust
Windy Gyle,
30 West Street, Belford,
Northumberland NE70 7QE
Tel/Fax: 01668 213 289
E-mail:trust@outdoor.demon.co.uk

Ballooning

Virgin Balloon Flights
Unit 1, Stafford Park 12,
Telford, Shropshire,TF3 3BJ
Tel: 01952 200141
Fax: 01952 290338

E-mail:james.ball@virgin.co.uk
www.virginballoonflights.com

Bird Watching

Field Studies Council
Preston Montford,
Montford Bridge, Shrewsbury,
Shropshire SY4 1HW
Tel: 01743 850 674
Fax: 01743 850 178
E-mail: fsc.headoffice@ukonline.co.uk

Bowling

English Bowling Association
Lyndhurst Road,
Worthing BN11 2AZ
Tel: 01903 820 222
Fax: 01903 820 444

Bungee Jumping

British Elastic Rope Sports Association
33a Canal Street,
Oxford OX2 6BQ
Tel: 01865 311 179
Fax: 01865 311 189

Calligraphy Courses

Acorn Activities
(see previous listing under Adventure Courses)

Camping

Camping and Caravanning UK Directory is the internet resource for camping and caravanning sites in the UK:
www.camping.uk-directory.com/

Canoeing

British Canoe Union
Adbolton Lane,
West Bridgford,
Nottingham NG2 5AS
Tel: 0115 982 1100

Car Racing and Rallying

For a comprehensive listing detailing venues that specialize in serious motor sports, ask for the *Starting in Motorsports* book priced at £3.00 from:

The RAC Motor Sports Association Ltd
Motor Sports House,
Riverside Park,
Colnbrook, Slough
Berkshire SL3 OHG
Tel: 01753 681 736
Fax: 01753 682 938

Brands Hatch Leisure Group
Fawkham, Longfield,
Kent DA3 8NG
Tel: 0990 125 250

Catamaran Sailing

Windsport International Action Centres
Central Information,
Mylor Yacht Harbour,

Falmouth, Cornwall TR11 5UF
Tel: 01326 376 191
Fax: 01326 376 192
E-mail:windsport.international
@btinternet.com
www.windsport-int.com

Caving

National Caving Association
C/o Monomark House,
27 Old Gloucester Street,
London WC1N 3XX
(written enquiries only)

Clay Pigeon Shooting

Dedes Hotel &
South West Shooting School
1-4 The Promenade, Ilfracombe,
Devon EX34 9BD
Tel: 01271 862 545
Fax: 01271 862 234

The Merton Hotel
28 Commercial Road,
Hereford HR1 2BD
Tel: 01432 265 925
Fax: 01432 354 983

Newland Hall also specialize in Stag & Hen Days with a whole range of activities:
Newland Hall
Roxwell, Chelmsford,
Essex CM1 4LH
Tel: 01245 231 010
Fax: 01245 231 463

Climbing

An informative web site covering all aspects of climbing is **Climbing UK**
www.eclimb.com/ukclimb/
Acorn Activities, Black Mountain Activities. (See previous listing under Adventure Courses) and **British Mountaineering Council** (See previous listing under Abseiling)

Comedy Clubs

The Comedy Store
1a Oxenden Street
London W1
Tel: 01426 914 433

Jongleurs: Central bookings
Tel: 0171 564 2500
Venues in: Battersea, Camden, Bow, Leicester, Oxford, Watford, Southampton and Nottingham

Cookery Weekends

Acorn Activities (see previous listing under Adventure Courses). Acorn run two-day courses where you'll learn a selection of vegetarian, meat and fish dishes. You can also go on a cider and wine-tasting weekend with visits to vineyards, plus full dinner and wine tasting on Saturday nights.

Cycling and Mountain Biking

Cyclists Touring Club
Cotterell House,
69 Meadrow, Godalming,
Surrey GU7 3HS
Tel: 01483 417 217
Fax: 01483 426 994
E-mail:cycling@ctc.org.uk

Dinghy Sailing

The Royal Yachting Association
is the national authority
for dinghy and yacht sailing,
motor cruising, windsurfing
and powerboat racing.
Royal Yachting Association
RYA House, Romsey Road,
Eastleigh, Hampshire SO50 9YA
Tel: 01703 627 400
Fax: 01703 629 924
E-mail:admin@rya.org.uk

Diving

British Sub Aqua Club
Telfords Quay, Ellesmere Port,
South Wirral, Cheshire L65 4FY
Tel: 0151 350 6200
Fax: 0151 350 6215
E-mail: bsac@.com

Drawing

Field Studies Council
Preston Montford,
Montford Bridge, Shrewsbury
Shropshire SY4 1HW
Tel: 01743 850 674
Fax: 01743 850 178

Acorn Activites and **HF Holidays** (See previous listing under Adventure Courses)

Dry Slope Skiing

English Ski Council
Queensway Mall,
The Cornbow,
Halesowen B63 4AJ
Tel: 0121 501 2314
Fax: 0121 585 6448

Calshot Activities Centre
Calshot Spit,
Fawley, Southampton,
Hampshire SO4 1BR
Tel: 01703 892077
Fax: 01703 891267

Farming

(See National Tourist Board's *Stay on a Farm* book published by Jarrold.)

Fishing

Acorn Activities (See previous listing under Adventure Courses)

Flower arranging

One day courses in practical floristry, fresh and dry flowers and tuition arranging bouquets, posies and sprays.

Acorn Activities (See previous listing under Adventure Courses)

Flying
The British Microlight Aircraft Association
Head Office BMAA
Bullring,
Deddington,
Banbury,
Oxon OX15 OTT
Tel: 01869 338888
Fax: 01869 337116
E-mail: bma@avnet.co.uk
www.avnet.co.uk/bmaa/bmaa.htm

Gambling
For a list of over 20 casinos:
Stakis Regency Casinos
Tel: 0171 833 1881

Gardening
One day courses available at **Acorn Activities** (See previous listing under Adventure Courses)

Go Karting
Playscape has tracks in Battersea and Streatham:
Playscape
Battersea Karts Raceway
Hester Road,
London SW11 4AN
Tel: 0171 801 0110
Fax: 0171 801 0111
www.playscape.co.uk

Gliding
British Gliding Association
Kimberly House,
Vaughan Way,
Leicester, LE1 4SE
Tel: 0116 253 1051
Fax: 0116 251 5939
E-mail: Bgahq@aol.com

Golf
For a wealth of information on everything related to golf, try these two web sites:
www.leisurehunt.com/
www.golfweb.co.uk

Greyhound Racing
Wimbledon Stadium
Tel: 0181 946 8000

Catford Stadium
Tel: 0181 690 8000

Wembley Stadium
Tel: 0181 902 8833 ext: 3412

Helicopter Flights
British Helicopter Advisory Board
Graham Suite,
Fairoaks Airport,
Chobham, Woking,
Surrey GU24 8HX
Tel: 01276 856 100
Fax: 01276 856 126
www.bhab.demon.co.uk

Holistic/Complete Indulgence

Foxhills Country Club arrange *Complete Indulgence Days* at the Foxgloves Health Spa. Residents of Foxhills Country Club have free access to tennis, 3 swimming pools, a 9 hole golf course and gym. There are 3 restaurants and 4 private dining rooms:
Foxhills Country Club
Stone Hill Road,
Ottershaw, Surrey KT16 0EL
Tel: 01932 872 050
Fax: 01932 875 200

Oakley Court Hotel is a splendid Gothic hotel with beautiful gardens, spa *(with a full compliment of beauty treatments)* plus leisure club including golf and tennis. Boat trips on the Thames available. There is a restaurant and private dining rooms:
Oakley Court Hotel
Windsor Road, Water Oakley,
Windsor, SL4 5UR
Tel: 01753 609 988
Fax: 01628 637011
E-mail: oakleyct@atlas.co.uk

The Sanctuary
A great health spa in the heart of Covent Garden.
11-12 Floral Street
London WC2E 9DH
Tel: 0171 420 5151
Fax:0171 497 0410

Wolfcastle Pottery offer creative pottery, coastal walks and aromatherapy for up to 12 people at one time at:
Wolfcastle Pottery
Pembrokeshire SA62 5LZ
Tel/Fax: 01437 741 609
www.pbiorg.uk

Horse Racing

The Jockey Club
42 Portman Square,
London W1H OEN
Tel: 0171 486 4921
E-mail:info@thejockeyclub.co.uk
www.thejockeyclub.co.uk

Horse Riding

The British Horse Society
Stoneleigh, Kenilworth,
Warwickshire CV8 2ZR
Tel: 01926 707 700
Fax: 01926 707 800
E-mail:enquiry@bhs.org.uk

Jet Skiing

Jet Ski UK also do Go Karting and Quad Biking.
Jet Ski UK
Lake 11, Spine Road,
Cotswold Water Park,

Cirencester, Glos GL7 6DF
Tel: 01285 861 345
Fax: 01285 861 828

Microlighting

The British Microlight Aircraft Association
Head Office, Bullring,
Deddington, Banbury,
Oxon OX15 OTT
Tel: 01869 338 888
Fax: 01869 337 116

Motorcross

Auto Cycle Union
Wood Street, Rugby,
Warwickshire CV21 2YX
Tel: 01788 540 519
Fax: 01788 573 585
E-mail:admin@acu.org.uk
www.acu.org.uk

Moutain Biking

Cyclists Touring Club
Cotterell House
69 Meadrow, Godalming
Surrey GU7 3HS
Tel/Fax: 01483 417217
E-mail: Cycling@ctc.org.uk
www.ctc.org.uk

Murder Mystery Weekends

Use your detective skills and try to solve the plot to reveal the murderer. Actors pose as guests, clues are dropped, the plot unfolds and it's up to you to say whodunnit.

Acorn Activities and **HF Holiday Ltd** (See previous listing under Adventure Courses)

National Trust Regional Offices

Northern Ireland
Tel: 01238 510 721
Fax: 01238 511 242
Wales
Tel: 01558 822 800
Fax: 01558 822 872
South England
Tel: 01372 453 401
Fax: 01372 452 023
North West England
Tel: 01539 435 599
Fax: 01539 435 353

Off Road Driving

The Federation of Off-road Driving Schools
Mandie Chester Bristow
PO Box 9, Hoyland, Barnsley,
South Yorks S74 OYY
Tel: 01226 748 822
Fax: 01226 740 151
E-mail: spectrum.cp@ao1.com

Paintball

The United Kingdom Paintballing Sports Federation
41 Cedar Road, Hutton,
Brentwood,Essex CM13 1NS

Parachuting

British Parachuting Association
5 Wharfway, Glen Parva,
Leicester LE2 9TF
Tel: 0116 278 5271
Fax: 0116 247 7662
E-mail:skydive@bpa.org.uk
www.bpa.org.uk

Wild Geese Sky-Diving Centre
116 Carrowreagh Road,
Garvagh, Coleraine,
Co. Londonderry BT51 5LQ
Tel: 01266 558 609
Fax: 01266 557 050

Paragliding

The British Hang-Gliding and Paragliding Association
The Old School Room,
Loughborough Road,
Leicester LE4 5PJ
Tel: 0116 261 1322
Fax: 0116 261 1323
E-mail: office@bhpa.co.uk
www.bhpa.co.uk

Performing Arts

For a comprehensive listings service of opera, concerts, theatre and ballet venues and events and gift ideas, go to the following sites:
www.whatsonstage.com/
www.lifestyle.co.uk/

Polo Clubs

For general enquires about polo:
www.polonet.co.uk

Scotland
Edinburgh Polo Club
Tel: 0131 449 6696
Fax: 0131 333 1331

England
Ascot Park Polo Club
Tel: 0134 462 1312

Potholing

National Caving Association
Monomark House,
27 Old Gloucester St,
London WC1N 3XX
E-mail: nca@ukonline.co.uk

Pottery

Acorn Activities (see previous listing under Adventure Courses)

Psychic

You can organize a host of psychic experiences including seances, tarot readings, crystal ball, astrology, palm readings at: **Mysteries** – London's Psychic Shop and New Age Centre:
Mysteries
9-11 Monmouth Street,
London WC2H 9DA
Tel: 0171 240 3688
Fax: 0171 240 4845

E-mail:events@mysteries.co.uk
www.mysteries.co.uk

Racquet Sports
To find your local club contact:
Lawn Tennis Association
The Queen's Club
Barons Court, West Kensington,
London W14 9EG
Tel: 0171 381 7000
Fax: 0171 381 3773

Rafting
Current Trends
Adbolton Lane, West Bridgford,
Nottingham NG2 5AS
Tel: 01159 818 844
Fax: 01159 822 033

The Scottish Rafting Association
Traditional rafting plus the latest sensation *Canadian Canoeing* (Old Red Indian Style canoes for up to 9 passengers !)
Scottish Voyageurs
Upper Wharf, Canal Side,
Fort Augustus,
Inverness-shire PH32 4AV
Tel: 01320 366 666
Fax: 01320 366 636

The Welsh Rafting Committee
Pioneer Activities
Waen Fawr, Pentrecelyn,
Ruthin, Denbighshire LL15 2HW
Tel/Fax: 01978 790 485
E-mail:pioneer.activities@virgin.net

Rambling
Ramblers' Association
1-5 Wandsworth Road,
London SW8 2XX
Tel: 0171 339 8500
Fax: 0171 339 8501

Rock Climbing
Outward Bound organize short breaks in rock climbing, walking, scrambling and mountaineering in a variety of different locations.
Outward Bound, Watermillock,
Penrith, Cumbria CA11 OJL
Tel: 0990 134 227
Fax: 0176 848 6983
E-mail:enquiries@outwardbound-uk.org
www.outwardbound-uk.org

Bowles Outdoor Centre is a purpose built centre an hour from London that offers activities including rock climbing /abseiling, canoeing, skiing, orienteering, ropes course, zip wire and problem solving.
Bowles Outdoor Centre
Eride Green, Tunbridge Wells,
Kent TN3 9LW
Tel: 01892 665 665
Fax: 01892 669 556

Sailing
See Windsport International Action Centres (see previous

listing under Catamaran Sailing)

Sculpture

Henry Moore's former assistant Peter Hibbard offers expert tuition in his own well equipped studio for weekend courses in clay modelling, rubber mould making, woodcarving and stonecarving.

Old School Arts Workshop
Top Cross, Midleham, Leyburn, North Yorkshire DL8 4QG
Tel: 01969 623 056

Snooker

Acorn Activities (See previous listing under Adventure Courses)

Snowboarding

English Ski Council
Queensway Mall,
The Cornbow,
Halesowen B63 4AJ
Tel: 0121 501 2314
Fax: 0121 585 6448

Surfing

British Surfing Association (BSA)
Champions Yard, Penzance,
Cornwall TR18 2TA
Tel: 01736 360 250
Fax: 01736 331 077

Tank Driving

The Activity Superstore
PO Box 123
Saffron,Walden, Essex CB10 1XX
Tel: 01799 526 526
Fax: 01799 526 528
E-mail:superstore@dial.pipex.com
www.serve.co.uk/superstore

Theme Parks

For an index of UK theme parks such as Chessington, Alton Towers and Butlin's, look at: www.leisurehunt.com/

Water Skiing

British Water Ski Federation
390 City Road,
London EC1V 2QA
Tel: 0171 833 2855
Fax: 0171 837 5879
E-mail:info@bwsf.co.uk
www.bwsf.co.uk

Wind Surfing

Lochore Meadows Windsurfing School
Lochore Meadows Country Park,
Crosshill, By Lochgelly,
Fife KY5 8BA
Tel: 01592 860 264
Fax: 01592 414 345

West Wales Windsurfing and Sailing
Dale, Nr Haverfordwest,
Pembrokeshire SA62 3RB
Tel/Fax: 01646 636 642

Rickmansworth Windsurfing and Canoeing Centre
The Aquadrome, Frogmore Lane,
Rickmansworth, Herts WD3 2DH
Tel/Fax: 01923 771 120

Yachting

Windsport International has sites throughout the UK which include water-skiing, sailing, surfing, canoeing, power-boating, yachting, tube riding, windsurfing and catamaran sailing.

Mylor Yacht Harbour
Falmouth, Cornwall TR11 5UF
Tel: 01326 376 191
Fax: 01326 376 192
E-mail: windsport.
international@btinternet.com
Web:/ www.windport-int.com

Yoga

Include a stamped addressed envelope for information on retreats and practitioners in your area to:

British Wheel of Yoga
1 Hamilton Place, Boston Road
Sleaford, Lincolnshire NG34 7ES
Tel/Fax: 01529 303233
E-mail: wheelyoga@aol.com
http://members.aol.com/wheelyoga

Tailor-made Trips

Trips abroad

The Air Travel Advisory Bureau gives details of agents selling competitively priced flights and on occasion accommodation to all destinations.
Tel: 0171 636 5000

International Train Enquires
Tel: 0990 848848

Amsterdam

Alternative Amsterdam
A website featuring Stag and Hen weekends to Amsterdam.
www.bus.co.uk/hotel-uk/amredlt.html

Amsterdam Express
Party coach weekender from Bournemouth via Southampton and Portsmouth to Amsterdam.
Amsterdam Express
203 Victory Business Centre,
Portsmouth, Hants PO1 1PJ
Tel: 0705 782222
E-mail:amstr@worldservice. powernet-int.co.uk

Club Med
106 Brompton Road,
London SW3 1JJ
Tel: 0171 581 1161
Fax: 0171 589 6086
www.clubmed.com

Eurostar

Plan a surprise ski trip for the bride-to-be, or regress to your childhood by taking the train to Disneyland Paris for a weekend!

Disneyland Paris
Tel: 0990 030303

Eurostar Ticket Office
102-104 Victoria Street,
London SW1 5JL
Tel: 0990 186186

Trips in the UK

National Railway Enquiries
Tel: 0345 484950

English Tourist Board
Thames Tower, Blacks Road,
Hammersmith, London W6 9EL
Tel: 0181 846 9000
Fax: 0181 563 0302
www.visitbritain.com

London Tourist Board
6th Floor, Glen House,
Stag Place, London SW1E 5LT
Tel: 0839 123456*
**Calls cost 45p per minute cheap rate, 50p per minute at all other times*

Scottish Tourist Board
23 Ravelston Terrace,
Edinburgh, EH4 3EU
Tel: 0131 332 2433
Fax: 0131 343 1513
www.holiday.scotland.net

Wales Tourist Board
1 Regent's Street,
London SW1Y 4XT
Tel: 0171 808 3838
Fax: 0171 808 3830
www.vistwales.com.uk

Youth Hostel Association
Trevelyan House,
8 St Stephens Hill,
St Albans AL1 2DY
Tel: 01727 845 047
Fax: 01727 844 126
E-mail:yhacustomerservice
@compuserve.com
www.yha.org.uk

Dublin

Dublin is becoming the Hen and Stag weekend destination. Bord Falite, the Irish Tourist Board, cites it as the most popular shortbreak destination in Europe.

Bord Failte (The Irish Tourist Board)
150 New Bond Street,
London W1Y OAQ
Tel: 0171 493 3201
Fax: 0171 493 9065

Edinburgh

Edinburgh Stag Weekends
600 Pubs, B & B to 5 star

accommodation, transport arranged with action and adventure activities catered for: paintballing, white water rafting, motor sports, flying activities.
Freephone: 0800 027 1011
www.bedlam.co.uk
E-mail: info@bedlam.co.uk

Specialist Companies

Healthy Venues
Specialists in arranging days or stays at health farms and spas,
Healthy Venues
45 Armorial Road,
Coventry CV3 6GH
Tel: 01203 690 300
Fax: 01203 690 400

Party Express
A company which has been organizing creative parties for over seven years. They've designed an unmissable *'Ladies Night'* – great for an evening out with the girls, even better for a Hen night.
Tel: 0171 630 6063
Fax: 0171 233 8474
www.partybus.co.uk

Awesome Events
Their motto is *'license to thrill'* and they organise Stag or Hen parties anywhere in the UK and overseas. Covering everything from tank driving to weekends in Amsterdam to table dancing.
Tel: 0171 233 5557
Fax: 0171 233 5260

The Weekend Company
Experienced organizers of Stag and Hen weekends. Activities include: tank driving, paintballing, micro-lighting, white water rafting, mountain biking, climbing/ abseiling, hang-gliding, rally cars, Formula Fords, golf, karting, canoeing, quad bikes, clay pigeon shooting, etc.
66 London Road
Nottingham NG2 3AW
Tel: 0115 985 1775
Fax: 0115 985 1795
E-mail:weekendcompany@compuserve.com

Zest-The Adventure Company
Tailor-made days covering a range of different activities.
PO Box 125
Richmond, Surrey TW10 6XE
Tel: 0181 255 4423
E-mail: zest@dial.pipex.com
www.zest-adventure.co.uk/zest

Hellish Presents

Ann Summers
The definitive name in naughty merchandise. Branches throughout the UK. Their web site has to be seen to be believed!
Head office at:
Gadoline House,
2 Godstone Road,
Whytelease,
Surrey,
CR3 OEA
To book a party telephone:
0181 645 8320
Order Line: 0181 645 8300
www.annsummers.com/

Stag Shop
To awaken your wildest fantasies, check out this great site.
www.stagshop.com

Rude Food Website Hall
If it's rude and it's food, this company probably makes it – from chocolate willies and condoms, to phallic bits of pasta. Check out the website and order over the net.
www.rudefood.com

Heavenly Presents

British Home Stores
For your nearest BHS department store contact the enquiry number: 0171 262 3288
Mail order: 0990 247 000

Ikea
For your nearest Ikea Furniture store contact the enquiry number: 0171 208 5600

House of Fraser
For your nearest House of Fraser store contact the enquiry number: 0171 963 2236

Harrods
Knightsbridge,
London SW1X 7XL
Tel: 0171 730 1234

The Chocolate Society
A one off membership fee of £50 invites your Hen to lots of chocolate dos and she'll receive a £50 hamper of quality chocolate plus a discount on future orders.
36 Elizabeth Street
London, SW1W 9NZ
Tel: 0171 259 9222
Fax: 0171 259 9666
Mail Order: 01423 322 230
www.chocolate.co.uk